*W*hat applicants shoul.

*B*e prepared for a lengthy time journey – to over 500 years ago. That was when knights built castles, took part in tournaments, enjoyed hunting and feasting, and fought (and died) in

wars. The map below shows your destination – medieval Europe, between AD 1000-1500. At that time, Europe was ruled by rival kings and princes, keen to capture each other's kingdoms. Most of their land was farmed by peasants, who grew crops of wheat and barley, and raised livestock. Goods were made by craftworkers at home and taken on horseback, in ox-carts or on foot to be sold in local market towns. Throughout Europe, the Christian Church was very powerful and priests, monks and nuns were the best-educated people in society.

Medieval Europe

Between AD 1000-1500

England

Germany

France

ASIA

Spain

Italy

MEDITERRANEAN SEA

Are you ready to fight?

Knights are expert fighting men. Do not think of applying to become one unless you feel sure that you could withstand a life of hardship and danger, and are prepared to suffer injuries and pain. You may even face an early death. But being a knight can bring rich rewards, such as castles, treasures and land. It is hard to beat the excitement of charging into battle alongside your trusted comrades. And what other career brings you the chance of fame, honour and glory that will survive for hundreds of years?

Aim high at the start of your career! Try to model your battlefield behaviour on famous knights like Sir Kay, Sir Lancelot or Sir Percival. They fought alongside legendary King Arthur as members of his Brotherhood of the Round Table. Their brave deeds are told by poets and minstrels in stories and songs.

Ready, willing and able

As a knight, you must always be ready to fight to defend your home, your family, your kingdom and your honour. You must also maintain a staff of grooms and squires (see bottom) to keep your horses, weapons and fighting equipment ready for use at any time.

6

Old and new knights

Traditionally, knights prize faithfulness and loyalty as much as fighting skills. Are you prepared to swear loyalty and devotion to your king (see left), even if it means losing your life?

Occasionally, you may meet a new kind of knight. He fights as a professional soldier for whoever will pay him, and even changes sides if he is offered a richer reward. He brings his own private army with him. Traditional knights do not approve of these mercenaries!

I will fight you to the death!

Knight and his staff, always ready for war

As a knight, you will have to get used to being called 'sir'. Being a knight is a sign of high social status. Some successful, wealthy men are made knights as a gesture of respect, even if they have never fought.

Are you from the right class?

Fighting is a man's job, so medieval women cannot become knights. You must be born a boy to stand a chance and everyone expects boys to be strong and brave. You'll be praised for boldness and daring – and blamed for showing any signs of cowardliness or weakness. You're also fortunate if your father is wealthy or a knight himself. Knights usually come from the privileged top ranks of society, although a few are promoted just for their fighting skills.

Medieval society is made up of a few rich, powerful people, and many poorer, less powerful ones. Compared with knights and other upper class people, like kings and lords, the majority have little (if any) power and are very poor.

5% of the population is made up of the king, nobles and knights.

5% is made up of merchants, lawyers and officials.

80% of the population are farmworkers, craft-workers or servants.

10% are the very poor, old and sick.

Son and heir

As a boy from a knight's family, you must do your duty from an early age. Sometimes this means spending long hours in adult company, rather than playing with your friends. But listen carefully to all that goes on – it's never too soon to start learning.

8

Girl or boy?

Your parents were very pleased when you were born. Male babies are always welcome, because they can inherit the family land and pass on the family name.

Something about brave knights and battles!

Joan of Arc

Occasionally a few women break society's rules, and ride off to war. One of the most famous women warriors was Joan of Arc. She lived in France from 1412-1431. She believed God sent her messages, telling her to lead the French army against English soldiers, who were occupying France. At first Joan won great victories, but she was captured and betrayed. The English had her tried as a heretic (false believer) and burnt her to death.

The Crusades

These are the wars fought against Muslims, for control of the holy city of Jerusalem in the Middle East. They began in 1096. Will you be a Crusader – a Christian knight?

For king and country

Your training will teach you how to behave in the king's service and while attending the royal court. You must be fiercely loyal to your king. He relies on knights to defend his kingdom. He may also call on you to go abroad, to conquer new lands.

9

Preparing to become a knight

Before you qualify as a knight, you will need many years of training. This is usually started at 8 years old and will continue until you are at least 21. Firstly, you must work in another knight's household as a page (helper) or a groom (stable-boy). You'll learn a lot about the good manners required of a knight, as well as useful information about war-horses. If you do well, you'll be promoted to squire. This is a responsible job. You act as a knight's trusted personal assistant, and even go with him to war.

You're very agile in that suit of armour.

Leaving home

Do you think you could bear to leave your home and family at a very young age to begin training as a knight?

Practice fighting skills and horsemanship at the quintain – a swinging weight on a tall pole.

10

Childhood training

Develop your fighting spirit by playing war-games with other boys. These toy knights (left), made of wood, will teach you the importance of fast footwork and strong defence.

Careful! This is only fighting practice – not the real thing!

Between the ages of 14 and 21 you will work as a squire, looking after a knight's war-clothes and weapons. Before battle, you help him put on his armour.

Special ceremonies

Some extra-brave warriors are made knights on the battlefield, but most young men have to go through three special ceremonies before becoming a knight. First they have a bath. This is not because they are dirty, but to purify their souls.

Then they spend a night in prayer at a church altar, asking God to bless their future career as a knight. Finally they are tapped on the shoulder with a sword by the king (or a senior noble) to make them into a knight. This is called 'accolade'.

11

Getting the right equipment

Becoming a knight can be very expensive. As well as providing a war-horse, weapons and armour for yourself, you also have to get equipped with a tent and baggage horses for use on campaign. For peacetime feasts, and for attending the royal court, you will need fine robes made of top-quality wool, silk or velvet and trimmed with fur. You will also need to provide some weapons, clothes and horses for the ordinary soldiers who go off to war with you.

If you come from a wealthy family, or have rich relations, getting all the required equipment should be easy. Maybe your father or grandfather will pass their fine robes, weapons and armour on to you. But if your family is poor, then you will have to capture them in battle, or win them as rewards.

That's an impressive suit of armour.

Armour technology has changed. Around AD 1000, knights wore suits of chain-mail (above left). Today, around 1400, knights wear armour plate (above right). You'll need a good set of weapons too: a mace, a spear, a long sword, daggers and a knife.

(a)

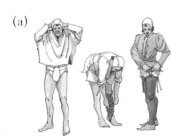

(b)

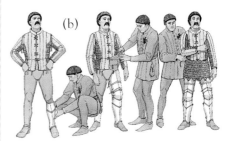

Your armour will protect you from top to toe. A helmet covers your head and a tunic, reinforced with chain-mail, guards your arms and shoulders. Your chest, back and elbows are shielded by metal plates as are your legs and feet. You'll wear a kilt of chain-mail or leather and metal gauntlets. All this armour can weigh up to 30 kg.

I have the sharpest sword in the kingdom, too!

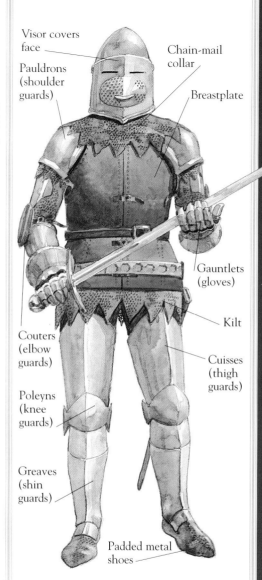

Visor covers face

Chain-mail collar

Pauldrons (shoulder guards)

Breastplate

Gauntlets (gloves)

Kilt

Couters (elbow guards)

Cuisses (thigh guards)

Poleyns (knee guards)

Greaves (shin guards)

Padded metal shoes

To get dressed in armour, you'll need help from your squire or groom. First of all, put on a wool or linen shirt, linen underpants, and woollen socks (a). Over these, wear your tunic and kilt (b). Then put on the plate-armour, being careful to fasten all its buckled straps (c). Finally, add your helmet and gauntlets.

13

Could you survive on campaign?

Expect to be away from home for many months when you are called up to fight in a war. Although each battle often lasts less than a day, it can take weeks for rival armies to come face to face. Medieval troops travel slowly – most of the soldiers go all the way on foot. Even if they have horses, they cannot cover more than around 40 km a day. Soldiers have to find food by raiding enemy territory, or by demanding forced 'gifts' from their own countrymen. Civilians hide in terror when an army marches by.

Spring and summer are the main fighting seasons, because muddy ground in winter makes travel difficult. Life in army camp can be tough. Could you cope with damp, smelly tents, disgusting food, dirty water, lice, fevers and rats?

On to the next village, men!

You may travel to war by ship, or even fight on board. When that happens, soldiers will jump from ship to ship and attack one another on deck.

On campaign, you need to take all your weapons, armour and supplies with you. Carry them on strong, sturdy pack-horses or mules (right).

14

Roads and bridges

When marching through enemy territory, you'll have to fight your way across well-defended bridges like this.

Stop! You've taken all we have!

Looting and pillaging

Looting is cruel and brutal, but most armies do it. You'll have to try and control your men. They will know that towns and cities offer the richest treasures to take away: gold and silver crosses from churches, fine wools, silks and furs from craftsmen's shops, and stores of jewels and gold coins belonging to rich merchants.

Soldiers in enemy territory will also attack defenceless peasant farmhouses like this (below). They'll hope to find food and drink there. As well as seizing any food stores, they'll also drive away cows and sheep in order to kill and eat them in camp.

15

Going into battle

No doubt about it, battlefields can be exciting. There's a terrific atmosphere as both sides pitch tents, make battle-plans, check their weapons and hurl shouts of defiance at one another. Before the battle, your leader will make a rousing speech, inspiring you with confidence in your own strength and skill, and increasing your will to win. But the fighting itself is horrible. Even if you survive unharmed, you will see many of your friends wounded or killed. Think seriously: could you cope?

If you get thrown from your horse in battle, you'll have to fight on foot to save your life. So be prepared! Get expert training in swordsmanship, to increase your speed and strength. Your survival may depend on your swordplay skills.

Foot-soldiers

You'll command troops of tough, brutal foot-soldiers like these. They fight with bows and arrows.

We will win because we are fighting for king and country!

You may be able to identify your opponents by the helmets they wear. (a) is a German helmet from around 1350; (b) is of Swiss origin at the same time; (c) is another German helmet made around 1370.

Arrows and lances

Longbows (left) fire a deadly rain of arrows on enemy troops. They terrify men and horses with their whistling sound. Knights charge into battle wielding long, heavy lances. They crash into ranks of enemy knights, hoping to knock them off their horses.

(a)   (b)   (c)

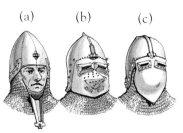

Crossbows are a new invention. They fire short metal bolts that can smash through armour. The bow-string is winched taut with a windlass.

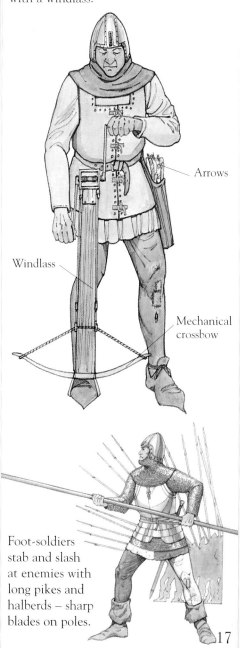

Arrows

Windlass

Mechanical crossbow

Foot-soldiers stab and slash at enemies with long pikes and halberds – sharp blades on poles.

17

Could you stand a siege?

*N*owadays, around 1400, most castles are built of stone, unlike earlier castles which were made of wood. This means that siege warfare is becoming ever more important. Do you think you could stand being on either side? During a siege, armies surround an enemy castle – or large city – and try to smash a way in using siege machines. If this fails, they simply stay around it and wait for food and water supplies inside to run out. Then the inhabitants are forced to surrender, or starve to death.

Sappers (miners) dig tunnels close to castle walls, then light fires in them (below). This causes the tunnel, and the wall above, to collapse.

Imagine being trapped inside a castle during a siege like this (below). It seems that you face almost certain death. But your soldiers try to fight off the enemy attacks and you send urgent messages by spies or carrier pigeons asking your allies to march to the castle and attack the besiegers from behind.

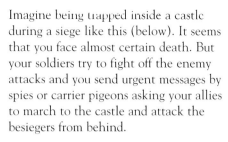

Metal cannon have been used since around AD 1300. They fire deadly cannon-balls, but are very dangerous to operate. Sometimes they explode, killing the soldiers nearby.

Plague

Besiegers hurl flea-infested dead rats towards their enemies, in the hope of spreading deadly plague bacteria.

War machines

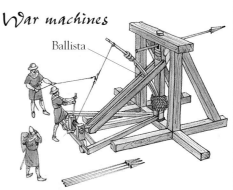

Ballista

This ballista fires huge arrows. It is operated by pulling back a big wooden lever then suddenly releasing it.

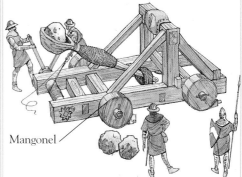

Mangonel

Catapults (also called mangonels) like this (above) are used to hurl heavy stones through the air, high over castle walls. They are operated by expert army engineers.

Keep attacking the battlements — the castle will soon be ours!

Trebuchets (right) are more powerful and accurate than catapults (above), but less mobile. Trebuchets can throw heavy stones (up to 50 kg) for almost 200 metres to smash holes in town or castle walls.

Trebuchet

Could you triumph in a tournament?

Tournaments are glamorous mock battles, and a favourite form of entertainment for knights, lords and ladies. They will provide you with a marvellous opportunity to win fame and glory, and rich prizes too, by 'unhorsing' your opponents while managing to stay safely in your own saddle. Tournaments began as a form of training for war and they can still be dangerous. Armed knights, mounted on armoured horses, charge headlong towards one another in the 'lists' – a special arena.

Tournaments are glittering social occasions – many important noblemen and women will attend. If invited to take part, you must look your best. Your shield should be decorated with your coat of arms. Originally signs to identify knights in battle, they are now badges of rank.

Both horses and knights wear surcoats over their armour, decorated with the knight's coat of arms. Tournament helmets have fancy crests on the top made of brightly painted 'cuir bouilli' – leather which has been boiled, to stiffen it.

Heraldic Crests

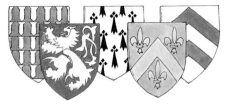

Tents

Knights taking part in the tournament, and important nobles, pitch their tents around the tournament field. Try to find time to visit each one, and politely pay your respects. It's a good way of getting to know important people who may be able to advance your career.

Wish me luck in the tournament.

Swords and lances are blunted and a central barrier stops the horses crashing into one another. However, knights taking part in tournaments often get hurt. Bruises and broken bones are common, as the participants fall to the ground.

Your girlfriend may give you her scarf or her glove, as a love-token. Wear it in your helmet with pride.

21

Rich rewards

*G*etting rich is not the main reason for becoming a knight, but you can win wonderful rewards if you are lucky in wartime. Your most profitable choice would be to capture important prisoners on the battlefield. Their families will pay huge sums to ransom them, and set them free. If you fight bravely for your king, he might reward you with gifts of houses, castles or land. You could perhaps try to seize treasures from houses and even churches in enemy lands – although this is strictly against the knight's code of honour.

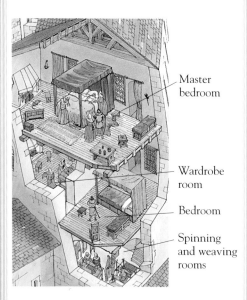

Master bedroom

Wardrobe room

Bedroom

Spinning and weaving rooms

Building a Castle

Capturing a castle, or amassing enough money to build one, is the most magnificent reward of all. It will stand proudly for centuries, as a monument to your strength and fighting skills.

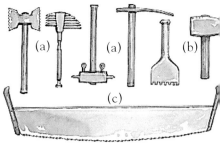

(a)   (a)   (b)

(c)

Solid foundations for a castle are very important to ensure it stands strong for years to come.

Men at Work

Master masons sketch castle designs on plaster drawing floors, and give instructions to building workers.

Workers cut blocks of building stone into shape (left), and (below) mix lime and sand to make mortar.

Carpenters make wooden frames to support arches while they are being built.

Plumbers cover castle roofs with lead sheets (right). Left: Masons' tools: (a) picks and axes for shaping stone; (b) hammer and chisel for dressing (decorating) stone; (c) saw for cutting.

What will you do in peacetime?

*E*ven the most warlike knight does not spend all his life fighting. To be a successful knight in peacetime, you will have to learn many skills. You may be expected to attend meetings of parliament or to advise the king at the royal court. In your local community, you must act as a host, giving feasts for neighbours and other important people. You must also help maintain law and order, and serve as a judge. Much of your time will also be spent giving orders to the men and women who manage the farms on your estate.

Poor people will stand outside your castle gate, asking for charity. As an honourable knight, you should help them.

More beer over here!

At the end of a busy day, your servants will welcome you home, bathe your feet and offer you food and drink.

Entertaining

When you have important guests, you must make sure that meals are served with great ceremony. Food for feasts should be finely decorated, or shaped into a surprise. At the end of the meal, you might offer them a 'subtlety' – a little edible statue, made of marzipan.

We've eaten well tonight!

Running your estate

You must preside at meetings of the village court, settling disputes between neighbours and punishing minor crimes.

The peasants on your estate live in small cottages with gardens where they grow vegetables and keep animals. In return for these homes, they work on your fields or pay you rent. You must check that all your tenants pay their taxes on time. Your servants must keep accurate records.

What will you do in your spare time?

Knights fight hard and they like to play energetically, too. You'll find that hunting wild boar and deer, and catching small birds with specially trained hawks, are a knight's favourite pastimes. Quieter entertainments include listening to music, reading and writing poetry, going for picnics and dancing. All these are enjoyed by knights' wives and daughters as well. If you want to please young ladies take care to have graceful, 'courtly' manners, and speak charming words of love.

If you enjoy poetry, music, song and flirtation, you will enjoy spending time with the ladies of the castle in their pleasure garden, with its grass-covered seats, flowers and pretty fountains. Sometimes they call it a 'garden of love'.

Hawking

It's a thrilling sight to watch a hawk swoop across the sky to snatch its prey. A well-trained hawk is very valuable, and a great status symbol, too. The right to own birds is controlled by law; only kings and nobles can keep the finest birds, such as peregrines and gerfalcons.

Music and dance

There's often dancing in the great hall, after the feasting is over. Do you know all the right steps for dances? Great lords will pay musicians to entertain their guests, but you might find it useful to learn how to play an instrument, to serenade your lady-love.

Visit a fair

On a fine summer's day, you might like to visit a local fair. Most villages have at least one a year, on a religious festival day. Stall-holders usually display their wares in the shelter of a castle's walls. Officials also keep order there, and look out for thieves and cheats.

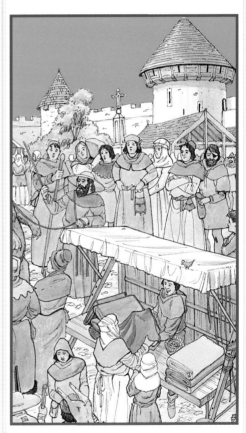

Outdoor Feast

After a busy morning's hunting, you may be invited to share a feast with a lord and his knights. Maybe noble ladies will join you, too.

Even though the lord's servants will prepare and serve the food at an open-air meal, it's wise to be as helpful and attentive as you can to the senior men, and to all the ladies. This shows that you have courtesy and good breeding – essentials for any young knight.

27

What are the long-term prospects?

A knight never gives up his pride in being a fighting man. But old age, aches and pains eventually stop him riding off to war. Many knights die young in battle but, if you are lucky enough to survive to old age, you will probably spend many hours thinking about death and the state of your soul. Consult doctors and herbalists, as they might be able to make you feel better. Perhaps you will give money to help the poor because the Church teaches that this is a holy thing to do. You must make your will and talk to priests about your funeral. Also, you will commission an artist to make a fine memorial for your tomb.

A good death

The Church expects knights – like all Christian people – to make a good death by bearing pain bravely, confessing their sins, pardoning their enemies and leaving money to good causes.

If you feel ill, doctors will remove some blood from your veins. They think this will make you better – it probably won't though!

Medieval remedies

Leeches clean wounds

Poultices soothe inflammation

Purges drive out poisons

Can you stop the bleeding?

Sisters of Mercy

If you fall ill away from home, you might be taken to a hospital, where nuns care for people who are poor or ill.

28

Herbal mixtures

Prayers for healing

Witchcraft and magic

He fought well but is badly wounded.

Tears and mourning

After you die, your body will be placed in a church or a castle chapel. Mourners will come to comfort your family and friends.

Burial

Priests will say prayers at your funeral service, then your body will be buried in the churchyard.

A lasting memorial

Ask a craftsman to carve a statue of you, as a memorial. Most knights choose to be portrayed as young, fit and wearing ornate armour. If you are married, you may want to include your wife on your memorial, too.

29

Your Interview

Answer these questions to test your knowledge, then look at the opposite page to find out if you have got the job.

Q1 Who do you feel most loyal towards?
A   Your best friend.
B   The king.
C   Your wife.

Q2 Where do you wear gauntlets?
A   Under your armour.
B   On your head.
C   On your hands.

Q3 What will you do in a castle siege?
A   Hide in the cellar.
B   Shelter in the chapel.
C   Attack the enemy from the battlements.

Q4 What are your favoured weapons?
A   Wooden clubs.
B   Swords and spears.
C   Bows and arrows.

Q5 How do you relax in your free time?
A   By hunting and hawking.
B   By painting pictures.
C   By gardening.

Q6 What are tournaments?
A   Kitchen gadgets that roast meat.
B   Mock battles, fought for fun.
C   Children's games.

Q7 What are a squire's duties?
A   He helps you put your armour on.
B   He sings in a church choir.
C   He acts as a spy.

Q8 What would you like on your tomb?
A   A plain stone slab.
B   A life-size statue of yourself.
C   A bunch of flowers.

Glossary

Chain mail Armour made of interlinked rings of metal.

Chivalry A code of good behaviour to be followed by knights. It involved bravery, honesty, loyalty and respect towards women.

Coat of arms A design worn on a shield or surcoat. Originally used to identify knights in battle. Later, it became a sign of high rank.

Crusades Wars fought between medieval knights and Muslim armies, from AD 1095 to around 1200. Each side wanted the right to rule the Holy Land – the area around the city of Jerusalem.

Estate The castle, land and farms belonging to a knight.

Gauntlets Jointed metal gloves worn as part of a suit of armour.

Oak-gall A growth found on oak trees, containing wasp larvae.

Poultice A warm, wet mixture (often oatmeal and water) used by medieval doctors to soothe swollen and aching limbs.

Purges Substances that were believed to make a person physically or spiritually clean.

Siege Surrounding an enemy castle or town and staying there until they surrender or food supplies run out and the inhabitants starve to death.

Squire Teenage boy training to become a knight. A knight's assistant, who helped him put on armour and learned how to fight.

Tournament A mock battle, fought for fun.

War-horse A very expensive, specially bred horse, ridden by knights in battle. War-horses had to be fast, brave and obedient.